T0158893

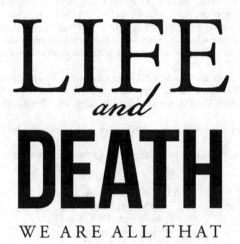

LIFE
and
DEATH

WE ARE ALL THAT

RONNIE FIGUEROA

BALBOA PRESS

A DIVISION OF HAY HOUSE

Scripture quotations marked NIV are taken from the Holy Bible, New
International Version©. NIV©. Copyright © 1973, 1978, 1984 by International
Bible Society. Used by permission of Zondervan. All rights reserved.

Scripture taken from the King James Version of the Bible.

Balboa Press books may be ordered through booksellers or by contacting:

Balboa Press
A Division of Hay House
1663 Liberty Drive
Bloomington, IN 47403
www.balboapress.com
1 (877) 407-4847

Because of the dynamic nature of the Internet, any web addresses or
links contained in this book may have changed since publication and
may no longer be valid. The views expressed in this work are solely those
of the author and do not necessarily reflect the views of the publisher,
and the publisher hereby disclaims any responsibility for them.

The author of this book does not dispense medical advice or prescribe the use
of any technique as a form of treatment for physical, emotional, or medical
problems without the advice of a physician, either directly or indirectly. The
intent of the author is only to offer information of a general nature to help
you in your quest for emotional and spiritual well-being. In the event you use
any of the information in this book for yourself, which is your constitutional
right, the author and the publisher assume no responsibility for your actions.

Any people depicted in stock imagery provided by Thinkstock are
models, and such images are being used for illustrative purposes only.
Certain stock imagery © Thinkstock.

Print information available on the last page.

ISBN: 978-1-5043-7433-0 (sc)
ISBN: 978-1-5043-7434-7 (e)

Library of Congress Control Number: 2017902187

Balboa Press rev. date: 06/05/2017

CONTENTS

CONTENTS

INTRODUCTION

Due to the consistency of what I feel Spirit is directing me toward, I will be writing about my beliefs and knowledge. My beliefs are much more open to correction than my knowledge. I in no way want you to take my feelings and beliefs as your truth, but I will attempt to make these concepts as clear as possible. Please find your truth from within yourself. I believe that the truth will resonate within you individually, as well as all of us collectively. I hope that, with the support of the words written within these pages, you find your true answers and your true self.

CHAPTER 1

We Must Live Now and Move Forward

From conception to birth and maybe before, we are all what life and death consist of. I will try to stay away from the mind-motivated speculations on the aspects of life and death and instead try to fill these pages with the heartfelt concepts I feel are more real and relevant.

To start with, we are all conditioned, to some degree or another, to believe what we have been told to believe. Even the ones who consider themselves gurus or enlightened beings are conditioned to some degree.

Spirit is all. You can call it God, divinity, love, the universe, the One, presence, awareness ... or whatever you want. The name is not as important as the connection we have to it. The connection to it is what we are all about. The connection to it is what death and life combine into and form.

All too often we hide from the importance of death rather than embrace both the concept of life and death. Some of us, out of fear of death, create religious systems to satiate the selfish part of our egos' need to believe that life after death is certain. This type of cover-up leads to all sorts of false ideas and suppresses the deeper fears we all possess. We rely on hours of chants or prayers or the promises of gurus that we will live forever, and it might be true. There may be an afterlife. There may be continuations of living on earth after death. Yet what is our true motivation? Does it come from the reality we allow ourselves to see from the depth of our being, or are we being motivated by a need to feel safe while here on earth?

Life Is Beautiful, as Is Death

Our minds create a gap that tells us that if we focus too much on death, we may very well die. Thus, it is best to avoid these kinds of thoughts like the plague, by shaking them off or, even more manipulatively, saying to ourselves and sometimes others that we need to practice thinking only positive thoughts. And I believe that, in essence, this is true, but it also can prevent us from considering all our thoughts in order to process which ones are generated from the selfish ego and which ones we need to be aware of.

I believe we must learn how to think about and even feel the experience of death in order to truly live. In the book *Advice on Dying: And Living a Better Life*, the Dalai Lama says,

"It is crucial to be mindful of death—to contemplate that you will not remain long in this life. If you are not aware of death, you will fail to take advantage of this special human life that you have already attained. It is meaningful since, based on it, important effects can be accomplished.

Analysis of death is not for the sake of becoming fearful but to appreciate this precious lifetime during which you can perform many important practices. Rather than being frightened, you need to reflect that when death comes, you will lose this good opportunity for practice. In this way contemplation of death will bring more energy to your practice.

You need to accept that death comes in the normal course of life."

Ecclesiastes 3:1–14 states,

"There is a time for everything, and a season for every activity under the heavens:
a time to be born and a time to die,

a time to plant and a time to uproot,
a time to kill and a time to heal,
a time to tear down and a time to build,
a time to weep and a time to laugh,
a time to mourn and a time to dance,
a time to scatter stones and a time to
gather them,
a time to embrace and a time to refrain
from embracing,
a time to search and a time to give up,
a time to keep and a time to throw away,
a time to tear and a time to mend,
a time to be silent and a time to speak,
a time to love and a time to hate,
a time for war and a time for peace.

What do workers gain from their toil? I have seen the burden God has placed upon the human race. He has made everything beautiful in time. He also has set eternity in the human heart, yet no one can fathom what God has done from beginning to end. I know that there is nothing better for people than to be happy and to do good while they live. Each of them may eat, drink, and find satisfaction in all their toil—this is the gift of God. Everything God does will endure forever."

The Quran states, "That you shall assuredly pass on

from one stage to another" (Al-Inshiqaq 84:19). Pretty heavy, huh? None of it needs to be overwhelming or scary. As we learn to live in awareness and presence, with loving intention, we see that it all makes sense, we walk in true acceptance and peace, and we become more and more in harmony with all that life has to offer. The practice is to let our deeper selves come up to the surface in order to accept the reality of our own and everyone else's death and not let the selfish ego unconsciously bury this reality within us. Acceptance and peace will follow as we consistently practice awareness and use the simple tools of looking deeply within, allowing ourselves to let all feelings and thoughts—whether they are good, bad, or ugly—rise to the surface. And with the help of Spirit, as well as other like-minded people, we can heal our past worldly conditioning and past trauma, which we all have to one degree or another. When more and more of us rise above the conditioned way of feeling and thinking, we will usher in what I call the collective shift.

Love and True Healing

We are born with an innate ability and desire to love and be loved. Much research and many testimonials have suggested this to be true. But how do we determine if our love is genuine and balanced? It happens as we connect more genuinely to our true selves, and it manifests itself in caring, giving, forgiveness, true grief, maintaining presence, and so forth.

Some might ask, "How do we know if it's real, and how do we maintain it?" What I have found is that as we practice awareness/focus/presence, other aspects of life become clearer, and things seem to work themselves out without too much interference from our selfishly motivated ego. We all have and need an ego. It is necessary for survival. The word *ego* means "a conscious, thinking person," and the ego enables us to use the tools that are available to survive.

It is what I call the selfish ego that gets in the way. That part of us manipulates us to look outside of ourselves instead of finding our truth from within. The selfish ego can be cunning and manipulative in order to maintain control. We all have within us aspects of the selfish ego. It tells us we are right and they are wrong, or they do not have the better way, but we do. We also sometimes use the selfish ego to protect ourselves from being emotionally or physical harmed. These unconsciously motivated actions can become our conditioned realities that we follow to protect ourselves. We reject others' ideas and instead continue to hide what we truly feel in order to maintain our safety. We do this individually, as well as globally.

We will swear by what groups tell us is true, and many will even die instead of taking a step to look deeper inside themselves for their own answers. As I mentioned earlier, we all have past traumas, to one degree or another, and we bury them in order to protect ourselves from emotional or physical harm. And as long as they are not healed from within, we will continue our existence, with continued wars and unnecessary deaths.

A friend of mine defined why we continue to

unconsciously hide our traumas. She called it "protective denial." The selfish ego will try to ensure that the individual or collective can continue its current path no matter the consequences. An extreme version of this would be the actions of those who feel killing people is right because of their beliefs. A subtler depiction of the selfish ego taking control is when we are adamant about something, and someone else is certain about the opposite point; then we begin to argue our beliefs over and over again, or even more subtly, we just give in to keep the peace. In order to heal and to help others, we need to break through the selfish ego's control, and we can do this only by what I call "living in the spaciousness of truth." This can be accomplished by practicing being in a state of spiritual awareness. And when we are living in this spaciousness, all other aspects of life become clearer, which gives us a clearer path toward understanding, accepting, and having more peace about death.

Some might be asking, "Well, how do we know if it's our more balanced selves or the selfish ego?" Well, we might notice that we become selfishly angry, or we begin to negatively judge others, or we become frustrated because we aren't getting our points across. As we consistently practice awareness, using tools of self-exploration, healing becomes more of a natural process.

And still others may be asking, "Does that mean there is no work involved?" True healing involves consistent work. That work, however, becomes a work of joy, dedication, and love, as we consistently bring ourselves back to this place of spacious awareness. Some of us try the next best technique if the one we've been using doesn't work. And still others settle for a relatively small degree of peace. Still worse, many believe that their techniques or systems are enough. There is no one technique, teaching, or religion that is going to help you maintain a truly balanced life. And don't get me wrong. If you are happy with the belief systems or tools you are using, then fine, but please see that only your own true answers from deep within will get you to the higher place of becoming balanced Human Beings. Our dualistic confusion results from thinking we must either work hard to achieve, or walk away from ego desire and trust the moment.

And to a degree, they both have merit.

The more you can stop focusing on which is the right way and which is the not-so-right way, you can focus more on practicing bringing yourself back to this place of spacious awareness, which causes presence and love to become more easily attainable. You will then find yourself being more easily directed, and true healing will occur. And when the selfish ego begins to fight back, which indeed it will, do not fight back; instead, bring all thoughts and emotions into this divine place of spacious awareness. Continue to use the tools that help you look deeper inside. This may cause you to initially feel worse than when you did not practice this simple principle, but by maintaining your focus, you will go forward through the crossroads and not deviate to the left or right or, worse still, remain at the crossroads or go backward.

We have an obligation to the world and ourselves to move forward together within this thing called life and death. What separates us is the fear of letting go of conditioned thinking, created by societies or spiritual leaders. And please don't get me wrong. I believe very strongly that there is much truth in what societies and spiritual leaders have taught us, and we will discover more of the collective truths as we practice bringing ourselves consistently back to the place of spacious awareness, along with presence and loving intention.

As we make the effort, the Spirit is always there to encourage another step forward. It may cause an event in our lives that helps us to let go of the selfish ego's control, or it may cause us to pray or meditate more consistently. When we begin to see the movement toward truth, we are hooked, and nothing else can easily manipulate us away from our own created truth. And the steps are not always pleasant. Please try not to hold on to the pacifying commentary of others, such as "It doesn't have to be painful. You can find constant bliss immediately." Is this true? Yes! Of course it is. Yet more often a statement like this is motivated from trying to extinguish the immediate pain and not letting the more natural course take its place. The more natural course will cause quicker and more lasting healing. Find people to whom you can open your heart, and let them help you break through the confusion with supportive spiritual interdependence. As you practice true healing, the pain that most of us encounter becomes less painful, and we are able to allow deeper realities to surface. And after a while, the old selfish ego gives up more and more.

Death is as important as life. By learning to live in the present, in a state of true awareness—with the acceptance of living and dying—love, peace, and joy will follow.

True healing occurs when we stop relying too much on others and instead heal from within. With the support of others you will find that spark of life that is uniquely yours—run with it. It may not look pretty; it may be riddled with errors. You may even at times go in the wrong direction, yet if you continue the practice of bringing yourself back to the place of spacious awareness, you and Spirit will continue toward a quicker and more lasting happiness, and a deeper acceptance and understanding of life and death. And am I saying that death is always going to be pleasant? No, I'm not. What I am saying is that we will begin to become more concerned about all the unnecessary deaths around the world, and we will become more empathetic toward all mankind. And with our collectives voices we will be able to help decrease the unnecessary deaths in our world.

Some of us deeply believe that there is a life after death, and some do not. It does not matter if you do or don't. I strongly believe that by living with a connection to our true selves, we will not fear death. We, as human beings, have too much of the *human* part in control, and too much of the *being* part of us is hidden. As we live this life of awareness, we become more balanced human beings.

Of course, as most of us have heard, it is important to not focus so much on doing, but instead focus more on being. It is even more important to not let any idea take precedence over your own unique learned internal voice. Then see for yourself if focusing on happiness, sadness, and so on is best for you.

True healing will make itself evident. The biggest hurdle will be the selfish ego, and next will be those who try to tell you how to do it. By consistently bringing everything into this spaciousness, which is you, you will excel. Above all else, just do it.

A lot of ideological principles try to explain how to become more of a spiritual person and how to tap into a power that will allow us to heal ourselves emotionally and physically, by virtue of an intelligent energy that manifests itself through metaphysical acts. Here are some definitions of "spiritual" from the *Merriam-Webster* dictionary:

1: of, relating to, consisting of, or affecting the spirit: incorporeal
2:          a: of or relating to sacred matters
             b: ecclesiastical rather than lay or temporal
3: concerned with religious values
4: related or joined in spirit
5: of or relating to supernatural beings or phenomena

Wow! That's a mouthful. Here's my definition of "spiritual": *an awareness of one's connection to an energy that is invisible, all-knowing, and everywhere.* The idea that an intelligent, omniscient power manifests material changes by desire, request, or intention is becoming more and more acceptable for many. Some people call these acts miracles or acts of synchronicity. Carl Jung coined the term "synchronicity." It means that if someone is in need of something, a manifestation will occur that coincides with what that person needed or thought. He called it "meaningful coincidences."

If you believe in a God or an energy that can help you, then you most likely believe that this energy can manifest itself by means of physical and emotional healing. If you accept all or part of what I'm saying, then you probably believe that if you connect with this energy, then the acts of synchronicity/miracles can occur more often. So why then (especially with all the significant increases of spiritual teachings, CDs, books, and seminars) are we not growing significantly more spiritually? Well, based on what I call "flowing spiritual logic," we are not connecting well enough to the energy source.

Why is this? Well, with all the spiritual tools we have, such as spiritual teachings, herbal remedies, meditation groups, yoga groups, spiritual seminars, and help from richer westernized spiritual gurus, it can become very difficult to process for ourselves. Our brains are wired to accept new information as just that, new information, and will not process it as the same old repetitive stuff we keep digesting. There is nothing new, and there is no secret to staying connected to Spirit. There is nothing wrong with going to seminars or reading the next new great spiritually relevant book. The problem is that we need to stick with a system that works initially and then continue growing with that system. Our minds tell us we need to have more and that we need to rely on the teachers and tools.

The tools, such as meditation, prayer, and group interactions are ways to get to the source, but not the source itself. Use what works best for you, and try to stick with that. My main point is that Spirit is in this place of spacious awareness. And with practice, we continue to grow more quickly and see permanent results. This creates a gap, which gives us the opportunity to heal conditioned hurts from our past. There is no need to work too hard at looking into the past or thinking about the future.

As you remain here in this spacious awareness, your thinking becomes clearer, you have more energy and motivation, and because of this clarity, you are able to plan better for your future. Hurts from the past begin to more readily reveal themselves, giving you the opportunity to release them. The release needs to allow the hurts to surface in the form of emotions, not so much thoughts. This allows you to heal more readily. And it's not about telling the feelings or thoughts to go away; it's about letting feelings and emotions arise and bathing them in this place of Spacious Awareness. You also will need to not let the selfish ego get in the way. It may tell you that there is no need to let past issues arise, but since we are all traumatized to one degree or another, we need to allow those emotions from the past to arise. We don't need to go looking for each and every past negative event, but we should allow those emotions to arise and bring them to this spacious awareness.

Some contemporary spiritual teachers insist that it is better not to use words like "negative" or "bad," but I disagree. I believe it is a bad thing to kill an innocent person or to hate one another. What makes the balance come to the forefront is when we can take responsibility for it all without anger, fear, or guilt and do what we can as a world to change ourselves and help the world change for the better. Try not to let the terminology shake you. Keep it simple, learn from within, and discern everything for yourself. Our thinking processes are so complex; it can be very difficult to maintain control of our thoughts. Emotions, on the other hand, are more specific, and we can more easily tap into them. Feelings of anger or fear are just that: feelings. You do not have to give a specific name to the emotion.

In other words, if it makes you feel bad, then practice releasing it. Do not worry; you cannot release positive spiritual awareness. Spirit naturally generates peace, love, and positive feelings and emotions. Sometimes our selfish ego can be so deceptive that we might believe that we have overcome our selfish ego and are as spiritual as we need to be. That is not being spiritual. That is being deceived. Be mindful of growing naturally and genuinely, and not making your selfish ego even stronger.

If you are truly connected to the source and experience spacious awareness more consistently, then you will continue to grow rapidly, and true love, peace, and happiness will surround all aspects of your life. One good way to discern if you are truly growing spiritually includes noting whether you relate better to all people, have less negative judgment, do not debate too much, have fewer mental distractions, have less of a need to be right, have positive relationships, and have the ability to not only accept death but also feel a balanced sense of peace.

Remember that we will always have a mind and body, and we will have positive and negative experiences all of our lives. We will only be perfect when we leave these bodies. So enjoy the moments. The presence and the releasing techniques I will show you will help you get closer to peace in a short period of time. Even if you do not attain all these things, your humble attempt is a most important factor. The genuine positive emotions will reveal themselves as you practice bringing yourself to spacious awareness and releasing. You have a Spirit inside of you, and it generates only love. It cannot get rid of itself. Therefore, no matter what you release, love and peace will remain.

When a negative emotion arises, bring it to this place of spacious awareness. The next simple step is to put a positive feeling in place of the emotion. Please do not let what I call the selfish ego say things like "Is this my ego or my Spirit self that is filling this space?" Who cares? By practicing being aware and releasing, the answers become clearer. If you are operating under a misconception, you will see it, and more readily be able to correct it. Try not to force or worry about the results. This incorporates the best of what you will find from the teachings that are out there.

Use the following steps to help guide you toward true healing:

1. Practice maintaining focused awareness and loving intention, even if for a few minutes each day. No matter how busy you are, you can find a time when you will not be distracted. And in order to condition the mind to consistently practice, it is important to find a similar time

to practice (such as taking a few minutes before bed each night).

2. Learn to become more aware of negative feelings rather than thoughts. Bringing all feelings and thoughts whether Good, Bad or Ugly into your body, focusing on the area in your body that it most effected. You might feel tired, so bring awareness to your tiredness. You might feel a pain, so bring awareness to that. Or you might feel wonderful, so bring focused awareness to the wonderful feeling. You might not be feeling anything at all, so bring awareness to that. And remember that you are more in this state of spacious awareness when you are more aware of the sounds or sensations around you and within you.

3. Learn to fully acknowledge/accept (not necessarily like) the emotion or feeling.

4. Release the emotion. You can say to the emotion or thought, "I am aware of you, I acknowledge you, and I release you from me now and forever." You can do this by using your own words or whatever tool that works best for you.

5. Replace the emotion with generalized positive feelings. You might say, "I now replace you

with loving intention," or "I am becoming more and more of a balanced human being." Continue repeating this until you feel better. You may not feel better immediately, but you will over a short period of time.

6. In order to head toward more immediate healing, share your deep feelings and thoughts with those around you. Does this mean blurting out every emotion or thought? No. It means that it is important to take the risk and share. You might start with a close friend, and then a group setting that promotes sharing, and then others.

That's it. You really don't need all the books, teachings, and so on. The healing is already within you. You need only come to a union with yourself in order to live a life with the One. Practice even if only for a few minutes each day. But practice as regularly as possible.

CHAPTER 4

Life

Life can be defined as the ever-present awareness of things that exist. When you are born, an awakening occurs throughout the whole universe. This same awakening occurs when you die. I also believe that if you meditate or let yourself be fully in a state of spacious awareness, you can experience in real-world time what it felt like to be born and then grow. I have allowed myself to regress back to the past, prior to birth, and while doing this, I have felt the warmth of a blanket. I have been aware of the size of my baby body. I have experienced various vivid movements all around me, and various emotions coming from somewhere else. As time after birth continued, I began to feel and hear those who were giving me attention. There was love, attention, anger, and fear. Our world has too much fear and anger and not enough attention and love. Even a lot of the love we think we have is combined with fear-based dependency and manipulation.

Throughout the ages, we have let ourselves be manipulated by lesser emotions. Is there a place for fear and anger? Yes, but not the kind we have created. Animals have fear and aggressive responses, yet those feelings are not trapped in their minds. they are a part of their evolution. We also have these genetically based conditioned drives which in and of themselves are needed for survival, yet relying on these realities too much has caused this planet to continue spiraling downward toward destruction.

Just for a moment think about how you feel when you witness someone brutalizing another human being. Do you feel anger, fear, helplessness, or maybe a desire to see the person punished for inflicting horror upon another? Or do you feel nothing at all?

At times, I have felt all those things. Those feelings are the opposite of what will cause healing.

The bigger problem is not those who inflict these atrocities, but those of us who do nothing to prevent them. It amazes me how we, as a species, continue to inflict such pain upon each other. I am concerned by how we stand idly by and do not attempt to stop the brutalities that exist. Ask yourself how often we pray for each other. How often do we volunteer to help? How often do we seriously just practice awareness, with presence and loving intention?

Does this mean we should run outside and give up all our possessions and go to a developing country to give whatever we can? Not necessarily. It means, however, that we need to be more actively aware of what Spirit wants us to do in order to give back on a moment-by-moment basis. If we live a life of awareness, then peace, love, and joy will resonate among us, no matter what the environmental situation is. And a more empathetic response will emanate from within ourselves and throughout the world.

More and more of us are evolving away from the conditioned responses and more into the more natural state, which makes it even more possible to use our minds, bodies, and awareness to heal ourselves and the world.

Moreover, we are ready and willing to experience a deeper evolution toward a more natural state, yet too many of us continue to be afraid to drop our guard enough to break through. And how can we break through? By being more and more in this state of spacious awareness.

I see too often those who believe they are experiencing true healing because of what their gurus have taught them, because of what they have read, and so on, yet those who are a little more discerning see that they are not growing as they need to. A more collectively spiritual group will be able to clearly see the deceptions, as well as the truths. The product of these groups will be true healing, and more significant manifestations will occur on a more regular basis.

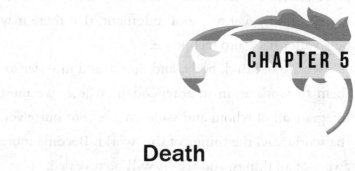

CHAPTER 5

Death

Who the heck wants to die? I don't! I think a desire to both die and be one with the universe is imbalanced. A true balance occurs when we live this life of awareness. Those who welcome death in this imbalanced way might be those who are willing to take their own lives, as well as others. There are also those who use death as a way to feel safe and secure, and not have to look at life as it is.

I recall feeling the loss and pain that comes from another leaving this planet. It was my feeling of loss. Those who left did not feel the same thing. The more we can learn to experience what death may be like, the more likely we are to find a blissful balance.

So where do we go when we pass on? *I do not know.* But I do know this: When I allow myself to have less or no judgment and fully feel that there may not be an afterlife, I have much peace. And also as I allow myself to fully feel, without judgment, that there may be an afterlife, I also feel peace.

We are of mind, body, and Spirit, and in order for them to work as an interdependent whole, we must integrate all of whom and what we are into ourselves, the world, and the things of this world. Become more aware of all things, and truths will be revealed.

Life seems to make more sense when we stop questioning too much (which we all do to some extent, whether we want to believe it or not) and begin taking the risk of trusting and following the true spiritual voice. And once again, how do we find this voice that will direct us to what is too much or too little attachment or desire? It is by living a life of awareness.

So anyway, back to *death*. Again, I believe that when we die, we shake the very fabric of the universe, and no one's death is insignificant. If we are all truly attached as one, then each death has meaning and affects each one of us.

Here is a practice you can try to help you experience death. It can be a profound and emotional experience. It might be wise to have someone available to speak to before and after the practice

1. Find one hour or so where you can be alone.
2. Prepare a warm bath, and quiet your mind as much as possible before practicing.
3. Sit or lie in the warm bath, and begin to visualize or imagine that you have died.
4. Let yourself experience various things that might happen, such as an obituary for you, or a burial. Experience the feelings that others might have because of your passing on.

If at any time the experience becomes too difficult, discontinue the practice. You can also modify this practice by lying on your bed, sitting in a shower, or doing something to give yourself a feeling of peace and solitude.

What is the most important step in this type of experience? It is letting go of the attached fears and conditioned thoughts about death. We are living to experience loving, giving, and enjoying the things of this world, and we need to learn to die from our fears and selfish ego–motivated conditioning.

CHAPTER 6

Groups

There is a divinely inspired movement happening on this planet. More and more of us are finding better ways to connect to the One, as well as understanding the concepts of that connection. Yet at the same time we are becoming more and more scattered and distanced from each other.

We are learning to be independent of the conditioned controls, which is a good thing, yet at the same time to be separated from the true union we need on this planet in order to truly heal ourselves and the planet. Even some new age teachers and gurus will say that you should not look to connect to the guru or the group and instead find your own way.

Yes, this is true. We need to not rely on the group or guru/teacher too much. At the same time, it is essential that we give of ourselves to a local community.

The smorgasbord of spiritual food also keeps many of us sampling every new healing technique, book, video, and/or philosophy that arises—not that these things are necessarily bad. Many tools are available to get us to who we truly are. My concern is that too many of us are relying on the tools and not our true nature. This happens when we let our selfish ego–based fears tell us we are doing the right thing by following a specific teaching, group, or philosophy. This selfish ego–based fear of being alone pushes us to join cults, follow the newest guru's techniques, or use drugs and call it a spiritual experience. All we need for true healing is what we were born with. That is our mind, body, and Spirit. When we learn how to use what we were born with, we can heal more readily, and we will gravitate toward the communities that are resonating more with truth.

Too many of us feel we have it so together that we do not need to join others to meditate, pray, and heal. Combined energy is more healing than autonomous efforts. When groups of people meditate and pray together, healing increases and crime decreases.

It is most important to first and foremost find truth within ourselves. When we discover truth within ourselves, we will resonate with the community to which we need to connect. Healing can occur more readily when people use their combined energies. A loving interdependent (not codependent) group is essential for not only individual healing and enlightenment but also universal healing. We need to learn to trust ourselves and the people to whom we are joined. This group will help us learn to have our own voice, as well as join together in openness, love, and trust.

The following is a good presentation of how communities may transform: People meditate, pray, sing, heal, and share encouraging words. People teach others how to become teachers and healers, they gather to meditate and pray for local and world change, and they initiate activities to encourage people to help change the world. It is important to have a structured format, yet there should not be a specific doctrine or dogma or even too much reliance on any one new concept.

And even though community groups are absolutely necessary for a true evolution, make the effort to resonate toward a group that will not take away your independence of Spirit. "Ye shall know them by their fruit" (Matthew 7:16). People of the new evolution will need to grow and change together. Some groups will continue to deviate from the true purpose, and all groups will in some way or another fall short of complete oneness. This is another unique way the universe keeps moving forward. Some look at this as the Yin Yang of reality. The opposing forces that bring balance.

CHAPTER 7

Saving Ourselves and This Planet

Today we use many techniques to enhance our lives and become closer to our true selves. There is no need to take years and years of practice to find your truer self. It just takes consistent practice of living in this state of Spacious Awareness.

The best tools to keep us aware and in the present are the ones we have within ourselves. There is no need for all the specific practices that so many groups use to help others heal. One group might say, "Practice this technique, and when you become a master at it, you will find enlightenment." Another might say, "Give your heart to the master, and you will eventually become a master with years and years of practice."

Think about it. How many lectures have you attended over the years? How many books have you read? And in how many groups have you participated? Specifically, have you spent many years of spiritual practice yet have not attained the higher level of one with the self?

The better answer I can come with is that *we are conditioned to believe what we are conditioned to believe.*

CHAPTER 8

Breaking It Down

The most important concept is to live a life of spacious awareness. The essence of awareness may have always been here, or maybe it was created—who knows? Either way, as evolving beings on this planet, we need continued growth in order to evolve toward enlightenment.

If you observe animals and insects without judgment, you might sense the unconditional acceptance they have to it all. In addition, if we stop the incessant thinking and let ourselves flow in a balanced way with it all, we begin to feel more peace, relaxation, and an awareness of the whole.

Awareness is the essence of all that is. Being truly aware is to be God. Stop for a moment, and observe everything you can. If other thoughts begin to take over, do not try to get rid of them; instead, observe the thoughts or feelings. Focus your attention on them.

Keep practicing bringing yourself back to observing it all. You may feel you are making too much of an effort, or not enough effort. Continue to practice and not let the feelings or thoughts of too much or too little effort stop you; instead, observe the feeling or thought of making too much effort, and continue doing what you are doing. The selfish ego will eventually begin to loosen control, and you, as the **observer**, will begin to be more of your true self. With this you can also in a positive way put love/giving onto all feelings and thoughts.

So what is the best way to know if you are truly following your true self and not a recording made by the selfish ego? Well, it's all about letting go and trusting the voice inside you. That is easier said than done, right (especially with all the conditioning that has been ingrained in us for all our lives, most likely even while in the womb)?

So how do we know if it's real or if it's not? The evidence will be in the life you live and the works you do. As you practice, it will make more sense to you. You will find yourself relying more and more on the life within. You will have more peace and love in your life, and you will give to others with a joyous heart, whether you recognize it or not. More importantly, you will find that you put less and less forced effort into your life

The best way to find the peace we all need is to bring out our reality. In other words, learn to be more honest with all that you are as a person. Even if you feel you are already there, know that everyone, to some degree or another, lacks the ability to fully be in touch with their truest selves.

That truest self can be called God, presence, the self, Spirit, and so on. It has many names, but it all boils down to the same reality: the truth is within us.

Is there an ABC format? Of course not. You may be at times practicing more presence or other times just being more aware, or a combination of both. Also, the negative feelings and thoughts you experience will be lessened by bringing yourself more and more into this state of Spacious Awareness. You will become more aware of unconscious feelings and thoughts, and you will begin to release them by virtue of being more in this state. Along with this, more acts of synchronicity/miracles will occur, and you will experience more physical and emotional healing.

CHAPTER 9

Conclusion

Okay, that's about it.

It is all about bringing yourself back to this place of *Spacious Awareness* and being aware of what you perceive, see, feel, or think in any given moment. When the questioner of the mind interrupts too much, bring yourself back to awareness. Try not to question if you are doing it right or wrong. Just do it, and you will evolve. You will know you are going in the right direction when you begin seeing yourself becoming more and more comfortable with yourself, no matter where you are or what you are doing. You will also know you are becoming more of your truer self as you see the continued acts of synchronicity/miracles occurring in your life. Find a group that is like-minded, and the evolution can be even quicker and with less pain or delay.

Practice a few minutes each day or as much as you can at bringing yourself back to this place of Spacious Awareness without forcing change. Try not to think it all through. You will evolve as you practice without much questioning or distractions from the selfish ego (although it will try its best). And keep pouring love/giving onto all feelings and thoughts, whether good, bad or ugly. "If you allow life, death, joy, and pain to be, then you will be free".